BEDTIME PRAYERS FOR CHILDREN

Illustrated with Adorable Animals

MAZ SCALES

Published by Fat Dog Publishing in 2016

First edition; First printing
Illustrations and design © 2016 Maz Scales
All rights reserved. No part of this book may be reproduced or transmitted in any form or by any means, including but not limited to information storage and retrieval systems, electronic, mechanical, photocopy, recording, etc. without written permission from the copyright holder.

ISBN: 978-1-943828-79-1

Before my words of prayer are said,

I close my eyes and bow my head.

I try to think to whom I pray,

And try to mean the words I say.

When it's time to go to bed,
Before I rest my sleepy head,

At the close of every day,
Lord, to Thee I kneel and pray.
Look upon Thy little child,
Look in love and mercy mild.

Be my guide in all I do,
Bless all those who love me too.
Amen.

The day is done, O God the Son,
Look down upon thy little one.
O Light of Light, keep me this night,
And shed round me, thy presence bright

Dear Father in heaven,
Look down from above.
Bless papa and mama,
And those whom I love.

Bless all the dear children,
In thy tender care,
And fit us for Heaven
To live with thee there.

As I lay me down to rest,
I pray my loved ones will be blessed.
God watch over me tonight,
Bless me with your love so bright.

The loving angels dance and sing,
And to me sweet dreams they bring.
When I awake to greet the day,
God I know you'll light the way.